THE STORY OF THE
TORONTO
RAPTORS

CREATIVE EDUCATION

Published by Creative Education
123 South Broad Street
Mankato, Minnesota 56001
Creative Education is an imprint of The Creative Company.

DESIGN AND PRODUCTION BY **EVANSDAY DESIGN**

PHOTOGRAPHS BY Getty Images (Allsport, Doug Armand, Scott
Cunningham / NBAE, Jonathan Daniel / Allsport, Garrett W.
Ellwood / NBAE, Sam Forencich / NBAE, Andy Hayt, Hulton
Archive, Jed Jacobsohn / Allsport, Robert Laberge, Fernando
Medina, Joe Murphy / NBAE, NBA Photo Library / NBAE, Robert
Skeoch / Allsport, Rick Stewart / ALLSPORT, Noren Trotman /
NBAE, Ron Turenne / NBAE)

LIBRARY OF CONGRESS CATALOGING-IN-PUBLICATION DATA

Gilbert, Sara.
The story of the Toronto Raptors / by Sara Gilbert.
p. cm. — (The NBA—a history of hoops)
ISBN-13: 978-1-58341-426-2
1. Toronto Raptors (Basketball team)—History—
Juvenile literature. I. Title. II. Series.

GV885.52.T67G55 2006
796.323'64'0975924—dc22 2005051766

First edition

9 8 7 6 5 4 3 2 1

COVER PHOTO: *Chris Bosh*

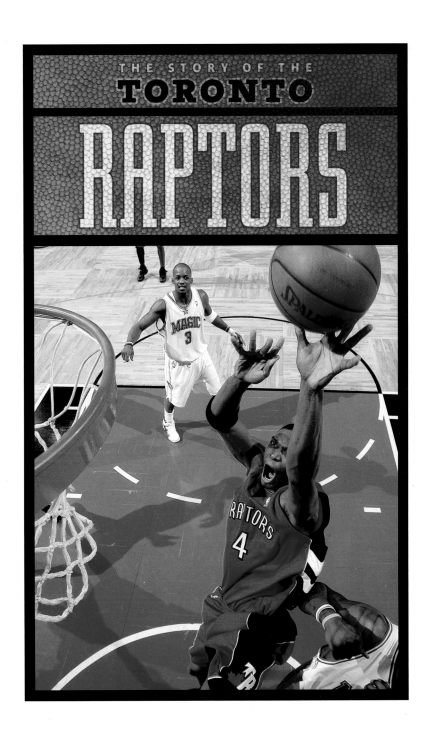

THE STORY OF THE
TORONTO
RAPTORS

SARA GILBERT

CREATIVE ● EDUCATION

There are no statistics

ABOUT HOW MANY MINUTES RAPTORS GUARD

VINCE CARTER SPENT SUSPENDED IN MIDAIR AT

TORONTO'S AIR CANADA CENTRE. BUT ANYONE WHO

HAD SEEN "VIN-SANITY" IN ACTION KNEW THAT HIS

LANKY LEGS WERE JUST AS LIKELY TO LEAVE THE

GROUND AS THEY WERE TO STAY PUT—ESPECIALLY

WHEN THE 6-FOOT-6 STAR GOT WITHIN JUMPING

RANGE OF THE HOOP. CARTER WOULD LEAP, ANGLE

HIS LEGS UP AND AROUND ANYONE BENEATH HIM,

AND SOAR IN FOR A SLAM DUNK. AND TO THE

DESPAIR OF THE RAPTORS' OPPONENTS, HE'D DO

IT OVER AND OVER AGAIN.

BASKETBALL GOES NORTH

1

TORONTO, ONTARIO, STARTED OUT IN 1793 AS A SMALL British fort along the shores of Lake Ontario, built to help protect Canada from a possible invasion by the recently independent United States. Since then, Toronto has grown into Canada's biggest and most influential city—one that has long been known as a hockey city. But in 1995, professional basketball came to town as well. That year, a new National Basketball Association (NBA) team named the Toronto Raptors was born.

Toronto businessman John Bitove Jr. had been a good amateur basketball player before establishing a successful investment firm, and he was determined to bring

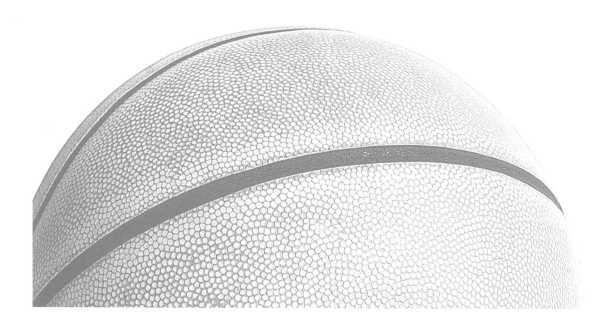

Big forward Oliver Miller was a key part of the Raptors' first season, averaging almost 13 points a game

Slick-passing rookie Damon Stoudemire finished fifth in the league in assists during the 1995–96 season

NBA

an NBA team to Toronto. After convincing NBA officials that fans existed in Toronto and putting together plans for a new arena, Bitove got his wish: The NBA officially granted the city an expansion franchise in November 1993.

The next step was finding a leader to help build the new Raptors. Bitove choose former Detroit Pistons star Isiah Thomas as vice president of basketball operations. Thomas, in turn, hired former Pistons assistant coach Brendan Malone as the Raptors' head coach. Then, in a 1995 NBA Expansion Draft, Toronto began building its roster with such players as forward Oliver Miller and guard Willie Anderson.

The Raptors next looked to the NBA Draft to find a point guard. With the seventh pick, the team selected 5-foot-10 Damon Stoudamire, who made up for his small stature with quickness, deadly outside shooting, and a fearless attitude. The young point guard had a tattoo of the cartoon character Mighty Mouse on his right arm. "Mighty Mouse was always saving people, always coming to the rescue," he explained. "He could get you out of any jam. That's what I always wanted to be like. Oh, and yeah, he was small."

In the team's first season, Stoudamire averaged 19 points and 9 assists per game and was the runaway winner of the NBA Rookie of the Year award. Even though the Raptors finished just 21–61, Toronto pulled off stunning victories over three of the NBA's most powerful teams: the Chicago Bulls, Orlando Magic, and Seattle SuperSonics.

BUILDING FOR SUCCESS

THE NEXT SEASON, STOUDAMIRE WAS JOINED BY Marcus Camby, whom the team selected with the second overall pick in the 1996 NBA Draft. John Calipari, Camby's coach at the University of Massachusetts, described the agile young forward as "a seven-footer with guard skills who blocks shots." Under new head coach Darrell Walker, the Raptors improved to 30–52 in 1996–97. Stoudamire established himself as one of the NBA's top point guards, and swingman Doug Christie ranked second in the league in steals.

13

RAPTORS

With his long arms and high-flying style, Marcus Camby was a top-notch shot blocker and inside scorer

A fierce defender, Doug Christie was usually matched up against opposing teams' most dangerous scorers

In the 1997 NBA Draft, the Raptors added another potential star: 18-year-old swingman Tracy McGrady from Mount Zion Christian Academy in North Carolina. McGrady's physical gifts were impossible to ignore. At 6-foot-8, he boasted a 44-inch vertical leap and was a superb ball handler. "[He] can be a great, great player in this league," said Indiana Pacers president Donnie Walsh. "He has the athleticism, and at his height, he'll be very hard to defend."

McGrady's first year was a turbulent time in Toronto. Early in 1997–98, Isiah Thomas resigned. Then the team was sold to an ownership group that also controlled the Toronto Maple Leafs professional hockey team. The new owners instated Butch Carter as head coach and made some blockbuster deals. Stoudamire and another player were traded away for three players and future draft picks, while forward Popeye Jones and two others went to the Boston Celtics in exchange for guards Chauncey Billups and Dee Brown.

These drastic changes destroyed the team chemistry that had been growing in Toronto. Christie, one of the few veteran players remaining, helped steady the team while McGrady and Camby developed, but the 1997–98 Raptors plummeted to 16–66.

RAPTORS RANK WITH FANS

When it came time to name his new NBA franchise in Toronto, owner John Bitove Jr. let the fans have a say. He put out a call for suggestions—and got more than 2,000 in return, including Beavers, Bobcats, Dragons, Grizzlies (which was used by an expansion team starting at the same time in Vancouver), Hogs (after Toronto's nickname, Hogtown), Scorpions, Tarantulas, Terriers, Towers, and T-Rex. The most popular suggestion was Raptors, fueled by the popularity of the 1993 hit movie *Jurassic Park*. Dino-fever was so hot that a month after the name and accompanying logo were unveiled, $20 million in Raptors gear had already been sold. By the end of 1994, months before the team's first game, Raptors merchandise was ranked seventh in the league in total sales.

PLAYOFFS NORTH OF THE BORDER

The 1999–00 NBA season ended with a momentous occasion for Canadian basketball fans: The Toronto Raptors, who finished the regular season 45–37—their first-ever winning record—hosted the first-ever NBA playoff game outside the United States. The Raptors had lost the first two games to the New York Knicks at Madison Square Garden when they returned to the Air Canada Centre on April 30, 2000, hoping that the noisy support of 19,996 Raptors fans would propel them to a win. Even though the Knicks won 87–80, the team appreciated the turnout. As the game ended, Tracy McGrady threw his sweatbands into the stands and walked off the court with his arms raised in appreciation. "I was just acknowledging the crowd," McGrady said. "They're the sixth man. They supported us well this season."

17

With his great wingspan and explosive jumping ability Tracy McGrady could get to the rim almost at will

RAPTORS

"AIR CANADA" LIFTS OFF

THE RAPTORS RECOGNIZED THAT THEY NEEDED TO add a steady veteran to help guide the team's developing players, and they needed to find a charismatic young star who could recapture the fans' interest. Toronto achieved its first goal in 1998 by trading Camby to the New York Knicks for veteran forward Charles Oakley. Then, with the fourth overall pick in the 1998 NBA Draft, the Raptors achieved their second goal. They selected forward Antawn Jamison, then traded him to the Golden State Warriors for cash and the rights to rookie swingman Vince Carter.

19

A 250-pound rock of a forward, Charles Oakley was known for his rebounding skill and bone-jarring picks

VINCE

20

The most electrifying dunker in the NBA, Vince Carter gave Toronto countless highlights in the late 1990s

Carter drew comparisons to former Chicago Bulls star Michael Jordan. Like Jordan, he stood 6-foot-6, shaved his head, and had played college ball at the University of North Carolina. And he could jump like Jordan. "Mike seemed to hang in the air a little longer, but Vince gets up higher," said Raptors forward Kevin Willis. "He'll come at anyone to prove they can't block his dunk."

Early in the 1998–99 season, the rebuilt Raptors moved into the Air Canada Centre, and fans packed the arena to watch Carter's high-flying exploits. Observers started calling him "half man, half amazing," and the Toronto faithful quickly dubbed him "Air Canada." Carter teamed up with McGrady— who happened to be a distant cousin—to give the Raptors one of the most promising young tandems in the league. Like Carter, McGrady had an explosive first step and vertical leap that allowed him to create shots for himself at any time.

Oakley and Willis, meanwhile, dominated the boards with a bruising style that perfectly complemented the Raptors' speedy backcourt. With Christie and long-range bomber Dee Brown helping as well, Toronto finished a respectable 23–27 during the lockout-shortened 1998–99 season.

COUSINS ON THE COURT

Vince Carter and Tracy McGrady met as teens playing Amateur Athletic Union (AAU) basketball in Florida. They became friends in North Carolina, where McGrady was attending Mount Zion Christian Academy and Carter was playing for the North Carolina Tarheels. Then they both turned up at the same family reunion, where they discovered that their grandmothers were distant cousins. Not long after that, McGrady and Carter became teammates. McGrady was drafted by the Raptors as an 18-year-old in 1997; Carter joined the team after a draft-day trade the following year. The cousins became almost inseparable in Toronto. They'd take turns leaping over opponents during games and then chat on their cell phones on the team bus afterwards. "They say they're cousins," said guard Dee Brown. "But Siamese twins is more like it."

RAPTORS RISING

4

BEFORE THE NEXT SEASON, TORONTO SIGNED VETERAN guards Dell Curry and Tyrone "Muggsy" Bogues and traded for forward Antonio Davis. These players gave the team the same selfless attitude as Charles Oakley, an intimidating enforcer who was happy to leave the spotlight to his young teammates as he took care of the dirty work down low. Combining these players' efforts with Carter and McGrady's high-flying heroics, the Raptors soared to a 45–37 record and made the 2000 playoffs. They were swept in the first round by the New York Knicks, but the experience was a big step for the young team.

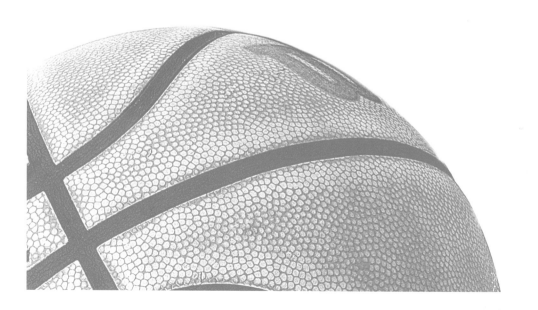

23

RAPTORS

Three-point specialist Dell Curry boosted the Raptors with his outside touch and smart, veteran leadership

24

Eric Montross and the Raptors finished the 2000–01 season with a 12–4 run and won their first playoff series

In the off-season, McGrady left town to join the Orlando Magic, and the team traded Doug Christie to the Sacramento Kings. The Raptors also made a change at head coach, replacing Butch Carter with Lenny Wilkens, the winningest coach in NBA history. "I'm excited about it, and I can't wait to get started," Wilkens told reporters. "I thought last year they made a tremendous stride in getting to the playoffs, and I think their future is all upward."

Wilkens was right. In 2000–01, the team started 26–23 and sent both Carter and forward Antonio Davis to the All-Star Game. A trio of trades that brought veteran forward Tracy Murray and center Eric Montross to the team helped the Raptors finish 47–35 and qualify for another trip to the playoffs.

Once again, the Raptors drew the Knicks in the first round. After New York won Game 1, Toronto fans feared a repeat of the previous season. But the Raptors rallied to win Game 2 by 20 points and sealed the series victory with a 93–89 win in Game 5 at Madison Square Garden. Toronto then pushed the Philadelphia 76ers to the limit in the second round, but the Raptors' season ended when Carter's potentially series-winning shot rolled off the rim in Game 7.

During the off-season, the Raptors welcomed a future Hall-of-Famer, bringing aging center Hakeem Olajuwon to town in a trade with the Houston Rockets. Unfortunately, the high-flying Carter missed about half of the 2001–02 season with a knee injury, and even though the team sneaked into the playoffs, the Detroit Pistons brought Toronto's season to an end in the first round.

BOSH BURSTS OUT

INJURIES TO CARTER AND DAVIS FURTHER SLOWED the Raptors' momentum in 2002–03. The team finished 24–58, out of playoff contention for the first time in three seasons. Former Pistons assistant Kevin O'Neill then took over as head coach with hopes of turning the team's top pick in the 2003 NBA Draft, Georgia Tech forward Chris Bosh, into a franchise player. Bosh exceeded the highest expectations, leading all NBA rookies in blocks and boards, but the Raptors did not. The team took a step backwards, missing the playoffs again with a final record of 33–49.

27

A star on the rise, 6-foot-10 forward Chris Bosh played his first game for the Raptors at the age of 19

RAPTORS

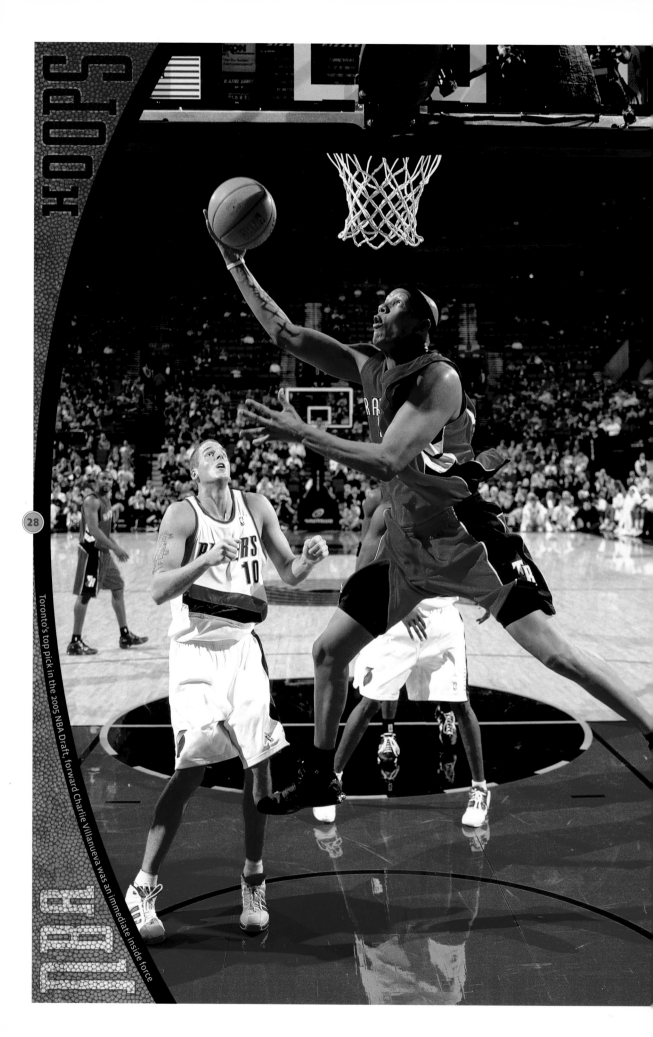

Toronto's top pick in the 2005 NBA Draft, forward Charlie Villanueva was an immediate inside force

The next season was a replay of the same story, ending with the same 33–49 record. Bosh led the team in rebounds with almost nine per game, and lanky guard Jalen Rose averaged 18 points per game to lead the scoring attack. The biggest headline of the season, though, was written on December 17, 2004, when the Raptors said good-bye to "Air Canada." Vince Carter had grown unhappy in Toronto, so the team sent him to the New Jersey Nets in exchange for forward Eric Williams and swingman Aaron Williams. "In Aaron and Eric Williams, we are acquiring two character players who are tough, defensive-minded players," Raptors general manager Rob Babcock said. "They will improve our defense and rebounding, and they fit the philosophy that we're establishing in Toronto."

In just a decade, the Toronto Raptors have risen from expansion roots to become one of the NBA's most exciting young teams. They have also captured the hearts of sports fans in a city where hockey has long been king. As Toronto heads into the 21st century, one thing is certain: like the dinosaur on the team's logo, the Raptors' days as an NBA doormat are a thing of the past.

AN OVERWHELMING ALL-STAR

Vince Carter was barely beyond his rookie season when, in 1999, he became the first Raptors player to start in an NBA All-Star Game after receiving 1.9 million fan votes. Carter was the top vote-getter the next two years as well, with 1.7 million and 1.4 million votes, respectively. In 2003–04, he received 2.1 million votes, the second-highest total in NBA history. A large part of Carter's appeal with fans across the continent was his spectacular dunking ability. In 2000, he won the Slam Dunk Contest with shots made up in midair, including one in which he dunked the ball, crammed his arm into the rim, and hung there as the audience sat in stunned silence. "The guy can hop," said teammate and contest finalist Tracy McGrady. "He's so creative. I've never seen that done before."

HOOPS IN A HOCKEY TOWN

Hockey is undeniably Canada's national sport, but basketball also has roots north of the American border. Basketball was invented by a Canadian, Dr. James Naismith, who introduced the game in Springfield, Massachusetts. The NBA's first game was played in Toronto on November 1, 1946, when the New York Knickerbockers defeated the Toronto Huskies 68–66 at the Maple Leaf Gardens. The Huskies lasted only one season, but 55 years later, the Raptors arrived. Toronto has appreciated the team, especially during the 2004–05 season, when the National Hockey League cancelled its season due to a lockout. The feeling was mutual. Throughout the final home game of the 2004–05 season, taped messages from Raptors players appeared on the Air Canada Centre scoreboard, thanking fans for their support and adding, "See you in October."

31

RAPTORS

Rangy guard Jalen Rose played for three other NBA teams before becoming the Raptors' offensive leader

INDEX